Talents Volume I

Talents
Volume I

Matthew 25:14-15

[14]For the kingdom of heaven is as a man
travelling into a far country,
who called his own servants, and delivered
unto them his goods.
[15]And unto one he gave five talents, to
another two, and to another one;
to every man according to his several
ability; and straightway took his journey.

———

Adeola B. Adeyemi

Talents Volume I
Copyright © 2008-2010 by Adeola B. Adeyemi
Published by Kingdom Light

All rights reserved. No part of this book may be reproduced, stored in a retrieval system, or transmitted in any form or by any means – electronic, mechanical, photocopy, recording, scanning, or other – except for brief quotations in critical reviews or articles without the prior written permission from the author.

ISBN-13: 978-0-98322-003-9
ISBN-10: 0-98322-003-4
Printed in USA

Kingdom Light
KingdomLightPublishers@gmail.com

All Scripture quotations are from the King James Version of the Bible.

For Speaking Engagements, Performance Requests, or all other correspondence please write to: TalentsVol1@gmail.com
http://talents.ws

Cover image: © Kristian Peetz | Dreamstime.com
Cover design: Adeola B. Adeyemi

Dedication

> "This Book is a multiplication of One Talent that was entrusted to me"
>
> ~*Adeola B. Adeyemi*

This Poetry Compilation is a collection of works over a span of 5 years of Divine Inspiration from Heaven.

All walks of Life can glean from these words of Hope, Faith, Inspiration, and Love. It is my Desire that as I present this Talent back to My Heavenly Father that the many eyes that behold it may come to know the Talent Giver.

Contents

Worship 1
   Prayer of Worship 3
   Created to Worship 5
   Tag Team Worship 7
   True Worship 9
   What Can I Say 10
   All Hail the King 11
   He Is 12
   I am Jehovah 14
   Oh How I'm Glad to Know Him 16
   Inner Witness 18
   Revelation 19
   Water Walker 21

Exhortation 23
   Be Still 25
   Habitual 27
   Trials and Tests 29
   Ordered 31
   In the Potters Hand 33
   The Message in the Tears 35
   Grace 40
   Dreams 42

Shake it Off	44
I Refuse	46
Roll Call	47

Interludes **49**

Mercy	51
In the Time of Adversity	52
Life	53
The Race does not go to the swift	54
Poetically Inclined	55

Love **57**

Eros 59

And so the Journey Begins	61
Beauty in View	64
It's only been a minute	65
If only one moment with you baby	67
Just thinking about you again	69
Masterpiece	71
On my mind	73
Sitting here	75
Beauty Composition 1:	76
Beauty Composition 2:	77
Beauty Composition 3:	78
Loving Eyes	79

Agape 81

Love 83

Unconditional 85

The Mystery called Love 87

Love…or Like…Love or Like Love…Or just Like 89

How you gonna sing about Love 92

The Search is Over 94

Salvation 97

The Battlefield 99

Prisoner to me no Longer 101

They Encounter 104

Armageddon 105

Valley of Decisions 108

Lamb of God 110

Altar Call 113

What does it really mean to be a Christian? 115

Call to Salvation

Acknowledgements

Worship

WORSHIP

Prayer of Worship

Father God,

We Worship You
In Spirit and Truth
We Bow to You
For You are Royalty

We Reverence You
The only wise Savior
We Honor You
For You are God

We Adore You
And Only You
We Glorify You
Give You all the Glory

We Magnify You
For all to see
We Speak well of You
For all to hear

We Praise You
For You are Worthy
We Raise You
High, and lift you up

We Bless You
For You are our Savior
We Thank You
With everything within us

TALENTS VOLUME I

We Love You
With all of our Heart

In Jesus Name
Amen.

WORSHIP

Created to Worship

Do you know Jesus
Creation knows its Creator
The Birds, they know Him
They Sing to Him in the Morning
The Flowers Magnify Him
They Blossom and Adore Him
The Waves, they Worship Him
Can you hear them roaring
And the Dew that falls
Do it for Him every morning

Just as the Eagle so full of His Glory
Can't keep from soaring
The trees they Praise Him
They lift their Branches
And Raise to Him
The Grass they wave to Him
They Bow down to His Majesty
The wind rushes
From his very Nostrils
The rain falls as showers
To mimic His Anointing Power

The Rocks Quake
Whenever He speaks
The Sun Rises
To behold Him

The Moon and Stars Glow
Because He holds them

TALENTS VOLUME I

The Seasons Change
To extol Him
The animals cry out
To personify a shout

But when Man encounters His Maker….
Words written on paper cannot describe….
Nor can anything in existence hide….or disguise

The sheer magnitude
There's no longitude or latitude
No distance
No instance in time
You see when Man knows Jesus
And His incredible love sublime
And how His own image is intertwined inside
Every cell, like a vine
Then He will find His Purpose
That all of Creation cannot mimic Man's Worship!

WORSHIP

Tag Team Worship (*Inspired by Isaiah 6*)

As we enter the throne room of Heaven
God's place of rest on Day Seven
You can't help but feel His Glory overwhelming
and the omnipresent flow of His Presence

The Lord High and lifted up
24-7 reverence
And a train that fills the temple
that nothing in existence can resemble

Above Him magnificent creatures were assembled
Seraphims with six wings
Two to cover their faces
so as not to look upon the God of Ages
Two to cover their feet
because the air they hover upon is the Mercy Seat
and two to fly

Already overwhelmed by this awe-inspiring sight
I struggle to stay upright which is impossible
For prostration is my only option,
to worship with all my might

And then with a loud voice one cries to another
The art of Tag Team Worship begins to uncover

"Holy, Holy, Holy, is the Lord of hosts, the whole earth is full of His Glory…"

TALENTS VOLUME I

another echoes as He faces another
Declaring together the Glory of the King
By the sheer magnitude of these words
Lateral communication produces a supernatural reverb
This sound of Worship begins to ring

For the door posts began to tremble
as the atmosphere achieves an automatic change of level
Smoke begins to fill Gods House
and the only word that I want to shout is.......

Holy!!!

That's all that can come out
Cuz like the angels I've seen His Glory
Matter of fact just look at the Whole Earth it's full of His Glory
This Heavenly example of what Heaven sees
can be reproduced on Earth, no
longer a mystery

For when men and women who believe gather
Telling each other who God is,
The Glory of God begins to flow
as the mighty rushing seas until all in the vicinity end up on their knees

This is Tag Team Worship!

WORSHIP

True Worship

To the Father, Son, and Holy Spirit:

As my tears soak this floor

Like the woman with the Alabaster box

Let my worth fill my Worship to you

Let the sound of my heart

breakthrough to the heavens,

To your throne, let my breaking

shatter my limitations

The Rivers of my inner emotion cause all of creation,

to respond to the emanation of my declaration,

I THIRST FOR YOU,

I THIRST FOR THE LIVING GOD,

I THIRST FOR MY LIVING SAVIOUR

and

every inclination of my living prostration

pours out to You!

What Can I Say

What can I say,
when you chose to die for me.
What can I say,
when you refused to open your mouth
in defense of yourself.
When you could have called Legions of Angels
to your help.

What can I say when I come before your presence,
when I know your body was broken and your skin was
torn with every stripe as each one of my sins tore into you
deeper than any knife.

What can I say when they spit on you and punched you in
your face.

What can I say as the blood drips down the crevices and
scars of your freshly battered shape.

What can I say as you took my place,
crucified in hands and feet,
so that I could escape the penalty of death
as your last
Breath tore me out of hell and into eternity.

What can I say Lord?
What can I say?
Where can I find the words to express what my heart
desires to say?
Jesus, Jesus, Jesus
What can I say?

WORSHIP
All Hail the King

All Hail The King
Glory is His Throne
Brightness is His countenance
A Richness that glistens like gold

A Radiant Power
So Great He Towers
And His anointing fills the Atmosphere
Like gentle rain showers
His robe made of clouds
And the light of the morning
Eyes burning like fire
A blaze that keeps on pouring
Hair that outshines the stars
And a train so majestic
Fills with no limits
Consuming every thing
With His Spirit

Son of God
Marvelous God
Glorious God
Beautiful God

Your Highness
Your Majesty
Your Holiness
Your Awesomeness
Your Excellency

He Is

He is my supplier
The one who brings in my chain
Jehovah Jireh
That's his everlasting Name
Higher than any height
On a different plain
He alone is God
A title only He can Claim

He is my Foundation
My sound Habitation
Jehovah Nissi
Chief Executive Officer of His Organization
He is my Head of which there is no imitation

He is my peace
My regulator
He lifts up my spirits
And so He's my Elevator
Jehovah Shammah
The One who stills my air
The King of Glory
He has made me an heir

He is my everlasting companion
My Comforter
He's always there
Jehovah Tsidkenu
With a track record of Faithfulness
That no one can compare
His loyalty is so Real
That's why His presence I know I can feel

WORSHIP

He is my physician
He created me
The mender of my physical
Not to mention my emotional, and spiritual
Jehovah Raphe
Healer so pure
He restores you to wholeness
Better than any cure

HE IS!

I AM JEHOVAH

How do you shake the feeling of disappointment,
the whispers of despair?

How do you weather the feelings of dissatisfaction in the air?

Or climb to the top when the stairs you are on
aren't going up, but spiraling downward instead.

How do you go on, knowing life isn't fair?
Knowing that you are where you are because,
your decisions got you there.

We all make mistakes right?

But why does it seem like mine, have taken me to a place too tough to bear ?

How do you encourage yourself when things seem so…
……..speechless…
So foggy and murky, so unclear ?

When the light of the dawn seems to be smothered by your tears

How do you get to answers, when questions only seem to spawn perpetually more questions; a Pandora's Box of question and inquiry.

Why are my eyes wide open and I still can't see?
Why are my chains broken but I still don't feel free?
Why do I feel so low and why isn't anything clear?

WORSHIP

To tell you the truth this is starting to become a burden too much to bear.

But then comes strength.

I hear a voice... "They that wait upon the Lord...The Joy of the Lord...Be Strong in the Lord...Not by might, not by power...Be strong and courageous...the strength of my life...I am the Lord I do not Fail...faithful...is there anything too hard for the Lord...He that has begun a good work in you will surely complete it……………………..……………..I AM"

I AM JEHOVAH JIREH I AM YOUR PROVIDER
I AM JEHOVAH SHALOM I AM THE LORD YOUR PEACE
I AM JEHOVAH TSIDKENU I AM THE LORD YOUR RIGHTEOUSNESS
I AM JEHOVAH NISSI I AM THE LORD YOUR BANNER
I AM JEHOVAH MEKADDESH I AM THE LORD WHO SANCTIFIES
I AM JEHOVAH ROHI I AM THE LORD YOUR SHEPPARD
I AM JEHOVAH SABAOTH I AM THE LORD OF HOSTS I AM THE LORD ALMIGHTY
I AM JEHOVAH SHAMMAH I AM THERE
I AM JEHOVAH
I AM GOD
I AM!!!!

Oh How I'm Glad to Know Him

To Know Him
The Lover of my Soul
To Know Him
Who contains Glory untold
Who loves me more than anything
Or anyone in this world
Oh How I'm Glad to Know Him

To Know Him
Whom all Power Belongs to
To Know Him
Who is Just and True
Who Cares about my Tears
The only One that can erase all Fears
Oh How I'm Glad to Know Him

To Know Him
The bearer of my Burdens
To Know Him
My Closest Friend
Who can Never Fail
Nor Forsake Me
The One that provides all Liberty
Oh How I'm Glad to Know Him

To Know Him
My Salvation
To Know Him
The God of all Revelation
Who possesses all understanding
The only wise God and

WORSHIP

Giver of all Blessings
Oh How I'm Glad to know Him

To Know Him
My firm Foundation
To Know Him
My Solid Rock
Who is a Strong Tower
Who controls Every Hour
Oh How I'm Glad to Know You….

Father God
Jesus
Holy Spirit

OH HOW I'M GLAD TO KNOW HIM

Inner Witness

Many times in life we must make decisions
split second choices that affect our mission
Moments clouded by truth and deception
and whichever way you go will teach you a life lesson

Sometimes these moments become so overwhelming
they get so frustrating
like someone who knows the answers and says
"I'm not telling"

But wouldn't it be wonderful to know what to do
because some of these decisions carry the weight of your breakthrough

Well there's this inner witness
this still small voice that won't force you to listen
an inner compass always pointing to the "Way"
an impression heavier than any weight
a knowing that's very hard to shake
Fed by obedience and
sensitive to every person's make

Inner Witness

Bearer of your directions

Inner Witness

Guide through your intersections

Inner Witness

Assurance of every move

Inner Witness

Insurance that you can't lose

Inner Witness

Your Only voice of Truth

Inner Witness

Revelation

When the impossible is within reach,
And the bottomless can be seen.
When hope is given substance,
And circumstantial participation,
Fails to intervene.

When cast lots and wild guesses,
Produce triumphs and successes.
When the relationship of boundaries
And limitations,
Get distorted like bad communication.
And what seemed to so easily disrupt,
Only leaves traces.

When frowns become smiles,
And displace what used to be stares.
And eyebrows go up,
Like petitions and prayers.
When hearts and attitudes,
Turn like winding stairs,
And attentions halt…
Become confined like babies in high chairs.

When the access to the soul,
begins to unwind.
Like business executives,
Toasting to New Wine,
And hardened minds
no longer Have to grind,
Because the chords are cut that used to bind.

TALENTS VOLUME I

When the lights go on,
it's easy to find
And things are understandable,
no need to rewind.
Purity becomes attainable,
key-word refine
An awareness of who you are, because it reminds
You of your inheritance,
Kings and Queens inside.

It Designs
It Defines
It Aligns
It Assigns
If you've ever been inspired, you know
It inspires
And burns within like fire
Sharper than a double-edged sword
I'm talking about the Word!

WORSHIP
Water Walker

What must it have been like for Peter to take that first step outta the boat?
I wonder what feeling was coursing through his bones.
What would possess a man to believe He could float, just by seeing another,
Well greater than another, Jesus the Son of God who spoke to him,
One word….

Come.

That's all he had to rely on.
I mean walking on water has never been done.
Red seas have been parted,
And Jordan Rivers divided.
Jericho walls have fallen ,
And chariots of fire have been sighted.
Raging furnaces of fire have been defied,
And Egyptian first born sons have died.
Lion's mouths have been denied.
Raging seas have been stilled,
And Goliaths have been killed.
But never has a man trampled on the mighty seas.
Or better yet with a word, caused another to imitate His feat.

This Jesus:
Who fed over 12,000 including men, woman and children, with loaves,
And cast out demons in droves.
The power of this man so amazing that terminal diseases would leave with a touch from his clothes.

He could easily make his mighty presence known.
Why do you think the bible says the heavens are his throne
And the earth is his footstool?
Walking on the water was just his normal routine of resting his feet.
And because now we are sitting in heavenly places with Christ Jesus,
We have a similar joint seat, to walk on anything that's underneath.
Because He's strong we're no longer weak.
Because He's overcome the world, all we have to do is speak…
To our mountains to be cast into the sea.
Because He's the Author we don't worry about the end,
Because He's Omega you'll become what he said.
Just look Up He's already ahead,
Bidding you to come walk on the water of your destiny.
Remember Jeremiah 29:11, He knows your
"Your expected end"
And Isaiah 40:31, "…You shall mount up with wings…"

Peter may not have known the magnitude of those steps
but he showed that if you trust, Jesus, and trust His word
you'll always be led
to do supernatural things

Like walk on water!

EXHORTATION

EXHORTATION

Be Still

Be Still
Don't move
He didn't say that you could choose
So hard
But a command
That you can't afford to refuse
A command that you may need to get used to
It may be the difference between whether you win or lose
Whether you at last get your breakthrough
For if you truly knew that He was God,
Then whenever He speaks to you to Be Still,
You will stop and Nod
For your trying to fight battles you weren't created to fight
Battles that you cannot win alone if you tried with all your might
Battles that are fixed…
Intended to Give Him Alone Glory
By moving you're attempting to rewrite your part in the story
An actor that rejects a script doesn't get the part
A sprinter waits for the gunshot, his signal to start
What gives you the right to undermine His authority?
Telling God, "no you be still, you can't do it better than me"
How can you even think that you can fight an enemy that you cannot see…
Alone…
Are you saying you deserve to sit on God's throne?
Well that's what happens when you disobey His command
Instead of doing all you can to stand
You keep the spot warm where you continually land

TALENTS VOLUME I

I know that not acting, letting go, we sometimes don't understand
But Obedience is better that sacrifice
And before you know it
He'll be raising your hands in Victory
Because all your enemies have become ancient history
All your mountains have been cast into the sea
And the path before you is now free
For you to proceed
So when God speaks, Be Still
Suppress your own will and Be Still!

EXHORTATION
Habitual

Why do I keep falling back into sin
Backsliding so much that I no longer slip in
on the slippery substance trying to make me fall
I willingly get on my butt without any interference at all.
When I would do right I do Wrong and that which I hate, I end up Doing.
When I know it's wrong I tend to redo
and that which is to be never revisited, I end up reviewing.

Which leads to this feeling of constantly losing...ground, of déjà vu
I thought I ONCE was lost but now I'm found
so I can't be found round and round, over and over again...or can I?
Maybe I keep forgetting my transformation
A sort of Spiritual Amnesia putting me in backwards motion
Got me so full of white noise, like a radio that can't tune into the signal of the right
station.

But then I consult the Manual of Truth
The only Compass that can be read in darkness
and shines like a beacon especially for you
And bright as day my path receives light
and my left of where I keep returning becomes my right:

"Forgetting those things which are behind, and reaching forth unto those things which are before, I press toward the mark for the prize of the High Calling of God in Christ Jesus"

And immediately I realize that's what I've been looking for
I kept falling into the same place because I had not learned
to seek the Word of God, His High Calling , and the prize
of taking Him at His Word.

To not dwell on my past mistakes and failures
but let God repair them like a personal tailor
Looking ahead to a future of Purpose
and laying aside every weight and sin because they're worthless.

I could not move forward until my faith increased
Faith comes by Hearing, and Hearing by the Word of God
So instead Habitual sin had to turn to Habitual Faith ....

EXHORTATION

Trials and Tests

Trials and Tests come to make you stronger
Temptation comes when you're forced to wait a little bit longer
When life starts to get harder
Grace stretches much farther
and Faith activates the pleasure of the Father

No more need to bring sacrifices to the altar
no need to negotiate or barter
No more thirst because He provides Living Water
that won't run dry
and Love that you cannot buy
Comfort so you don't have to cry
and Life Everlasting so you don't have to die

Your life is pre-destined so no need to improvise
just get a hold of Scripture, Your-Script
and you can't be surprised
because when the adversary comes to sift
You'll already know the answers and how to reply

For the Word, sharper than any double-edged sword, hidden in your heart
Equipped to counteract the fiery darts
and the smooth deception
and give you peace as well as provide protection
Not to mention the many blessings
and benefits that we don't deserve
free of charge

TALENTS VOLUME I

All He asks is that we serve Him Only
And Love Him Totally
Giving Him Glory
Worship Him Solely
Because He Alone is Holy

EXHORTATION

Ordered

My steps are ordered
My steps are ordered of God
Intricately and delicately placed
Way before I entered into this race

For He set which foot would be right
and which would be left
Right down to the conditions
Whether I would walk in day or night
The grade before I took the test

Through the rain
or through the fire
through the storm
or simply when I'm tired

I may not understand where you're taking me
Because I only can calculate what I can see

But when what I see is new
my mind becomes confused
I don't have a clue
So foggy, so cloudy

Thinking I'm lost
I can't even see that Jesus is right beside me
I think I'm wandering blindly
but my feet have been ordered

Before I existed
my feet were given the coordinates
A commandment from the Father, an ordinance

TALENTS VOLUME I

to follow the invisible lamp,
the direction in the path
To get my strength form thy rod and thy staff

You see the sheep always hear the Sheppard's voice
They have free will and choice
but their feet don't wait, they take steps closer...
Just following Order

The times when my feet leave the ground
I hear footsteps of another
but nobody's around
I'm moving forward
Then I realize someone's carrying me
He whispers a sound into my ear...

Ordered

EXHORTATION
In the Potters Hand

The manifestation of His Glory to light up your Lane.
The manifestation of His Presence to remind you it's not in vain.
So what now can we say to these things,
If God be for us who can be against us.
And what weight do you think you need to bring,
when in Him is all you need to trust.
Tears running down your cheeks clasping hands under your chin,
pain so evident you wouldn't believe it's from within.
Why, has become the only language that you speak,
because any other words will remind your heart to skip a beat.
Because the negative thoughts and memories will only seem to repeat,
feelings of rejection, hurt, you thought you'll never see.
Anger and Unforgiveness,
"I never thought it would be me?"

What does God think, what would He say?
I do not know cuz I refuse to pray.
I'm supposed to be a Christian,
that's what people will say. Am I not human, can I be imperfect, if only for one day?
The fact of the matter is at this moment, it's hard keeping the flesh at bay.

Lord why did things have to end up this way?
I know you're the Potter and I'm the clay,
but why does it seem like I keep falling off your tray?
Like you've allowed someone to take me and leave me out in the sun to waste away?

TALENTS VOLUME I

My Form keeps changing with every impact I make,
assuming the shape of every storm I face; not to
mention the fire that's blazing,
taking me from solid to
liquid, sometimes
I think I'm going crazy.

But maybe it's just the refiner's fire,
that's separating me from the impurities.
Sins and faults that ruin my value that only
the increased temperature can reveal.
Burning up the unwanted and leaving gold intact,
returning me to the mold,
your original intent,
that's stamped with your seal of approval.
Cuz when you're done and the clay is dry,
I'll be steadfast and unmovable.

EXHORTATION
The Message In The Tears

Dear God,
Tomorrow's the first of the month
The rent is due, the light and gas too
I know I don't have enough
I don't know what to do
My little boy is seven and my baby girl is just two
I can't let them know that mommy can't afford food

...since He left me, I can't even afford new shoes and
it's only a matter of time before they catch a clue
before they start asking mommy why isn't daddy here
Mommy why is your face always covered in tears?

I see them, then order them
I read them, then store them

Dear God,
If you really are listening, you really are up there
I'm not sure I want to go on living anymore, do you even care
Why would you let Him violate me like this, did you hear my prayer?
I never thought it would be me, how could my daddy molest me...
It's still hard to believe, I begged him to stop
I cried daddy please...but he wouldn't...
Night after night trampling on my innocence...
How could a man want me now, how could anyone love this mess of a woman?
How do I go on through this life slipping and sliding on these rivers of tears I've shed?

TALENTS VOLUME I

I see them, then order them
I read them, then store them

Dear God,
This is starting to take a toll on me, these strangers, these women that have graced my bedspread. I thought it was the good life
A different lady each week, I said to myself, "I don't need a wife"
But
It's getting to be too many to count…
I can't seem to get out.
I enjoyed the way they made me feel, the momentary thrills
but it seems like my mornings are filled
with a deeper hunger that my nights haven't fulfilled.
The emptiness is still there,
The yearning is still there,
The void has never ceased to be there
And now I can admit I'm scared.
I remember my momma talking about a Love unconditional, she said you could put it there but I thought, I thought you wouldn't care.
After the 10th woman I, I thought You wouldn't even bear to look at me…
I couldn't even look at me, so I ran away from prayer…until today
Because you see I'm so desperately in need of you.
I admit I've been a fool…
I've always heard that men don't cry
But if that were true what are these tears falling from my eyes, can you deliver me from this state, is it too late?

EXHORTATION

I see them, I order them
I read them, then store them

My Children
My Children
I've read your tears
The prayers, unspeakable, unutterable
That only I could hear

I kept them here in my hand
My tears mixed with yours

As I collected them, mines began to pour
Yours are but droplets, mines are like showers
But don't misunderstand I have the power,
I cried because as Jesus, I understand

Single Mother I understand
Be strong, because I am holding your hand
I am a Father to the Fatherless
I'll never leave I'll always be there
I'll supply all your needs, I've even numbered your hairs
I've wrapped your son and your daughter
with my Love from toe to head,
I've never left the righteous forsaken,
nor their seed begging bread
And don't worry this daddy isn't going nowhere

My daughter, my Will wasn't for you to go through such pain
I heard your prayer, I know your name
For I want you to know the thoughts that I think toward you, of peace not of evil, to give you an expected end

TALENTS VOLUME I

I've gathered the pieces of your life, which only I can mend
You will Live, you were fearfully and wonderfully made
I will restore to you the years that your daddy made you afraid,
I will repay,
you will reclaim Joy for your shame, Peace that you can't explain, and healing like rain
For as long as you put your trust in me no one will ever hurt you again

My Son, my precious son, I've never refrained from extending my arms to you
I wish you could know how I've longed that you would turn to me, and see that I am what you need
My greatest desire is for you to know that
Before I formed you in the womb I knew and approved of you as mine,
and before you were born I separated and set you apart to shine
I hold that missing piece of your heart
You're the apple of my eye there's no one above you
Before the World was I Loved you
I desire that your joy may be full
and no I don't consider you a fool
My blood has made you pleasing in my sight
Forget the past my righteousness has made you right
Come unto me I will give you rest
My yoke is easy my burden is light,
I declare this your Day, This is the end of your night

My Daughters, My Sons, Make sure you hear
I alone can vanquish your fears
You're not alone because I'm always near

EXHORTATION

I'll never put more on you than you can bear
Cast your burdens onto me for I care, I care
I am God,
I'm the only one
who can read
the message in your tears

(Every Tear-drop contains a detailed Biography of what you're going through, Jesus cares enough To read everyone that falls from your eyes, why don't you give Him Your Life and Make Him your Personal Saviour, Jesus Loves You!)

GRACE

Oh Lord I Need Your Grace
That Brings Me before Your Face
On My Knees Because I Realize How Much I Need You...

Grace

That Helps Me Finish This Race
Your Grace
That Makes Me Strong When I Am Weak
Your Grace
That Does Erase Every Hint of Sin And
Makes Me Entirely Worthy
That Takes Me from a Pawn to an Ace

Oh Lord Jesus I Need Your Grace
that takes your royal lace and
covers me in Righteousness and praise
Undeserved

Grace

Oh Lord I need your Grace
that breaks every temptation
because your strength is made perfect
I need your grace
Grace that measures out sanctification
until our spirits leave this earthly place
Grace that strengthens my foundation
when the enemy decides to storm this base

EXHORTATION

Oh Lord how much I need your grace that is patient to
work with me hourly, case by case
Grace that keeps me on this race on a heavenly pace
Oh Lord Jesus I need your Grace
because your Grace, Grace
will leave these mountains in waste

Oh Lord
I Need
Your
GRACE!

Dreams

Dreams are meant to touch and take hold of the impossible.
Tear down any mountain, any road, any obstacle.
Be as outrageous as numbering every one of your hair follicles,
and as attainable as gathering up water molecules.

So why do some dreams seem so diabolical?
All they do is rob you of vitality and essence,
and all you seem to gain is lesson after lesson.

Why do some dreams seem so unmethodical?
Like understanding the etiological history of man,
and some so obvious like hitting a baseball into the stands.

Why can some flow freely,
while others demand?
Why do some always seem like they can't ever fit in your hand?
Why are they so hard to understand?
Like trying to make a steel ball expand.

Dreams can bring into existence.
Can make a blind man see and a deaf man listen.
Turn a thug into a business man,
and keep an impoverished child wishing.
Can take a raped child like Oprah,
and make here one of the riches women living.

EXHORTATION

Dreams can turn a crack house into a studio,
and a street corner into a dance floor.
Dreams can flip our definition of great,
like turning an ocean into a lake.

When we go to sleep, dreams are what we make.
Embrace and live by until we awake.
Feed on like a fat kid on cake.
Powers and drives us because our lives are at stake.
Keeps us grounded for sanity's sake.

But for a dream to be effective and not be fake,
you gotta have the same dream when you're sleeping,
and when you're awake.

Shake it Off

Don't just sit there, shake it off
Don't just stand there, take off
When you want to get your throat clear, you cough
So when something you don't want is on you, shake it off

If at first you don't succeed, check what you're carrying
a lot of times what you're wearing affects your speed
Where you're going you can't afford delays
So audit yourself and shake off what you don't need

Sometimes baggage wants to hold on
leech your patience, happiness and drive
Be that stumbling block, that slippery slope
that affects your climb

Examine yourself
The unexamined life isn't worth living
No purpose
No direction
You don't know yourself
and that's what's keeping you sitting

Shake yourself loose and start believing
Give and you shall keep receiving
Keep digging until you start retrieving
Don't just succeed, start superseding

Shake up your situation, like a wet dog getting dry
Shake off the cold and begin to fly
Shake off that individual, leave them behind
Shake off that delay, you have enough time
Shake off that memory of what someone said

EXHORTATION

Shake off those tears you shed
Shake off whatever is keeping you from moving ahead
Sometimes you've gotta do the majority of shaking in your head

Don't worry, Don't fear, Don't doubt, Don't get angry

Shake it off instead!

I Refuse

I refuse to stick to the norm
I'd rather fly solo then go with the swarm
For inside this vessel dreams are borne
shoes that have never been worn
I refuse to reach for the sky
cuz that puts limits on how High i can fly

I refuse to let anyone get the best of me
to hold me down and keep me from being free
I refuse to live life insignificantly
to walk through life aimlessly
nonchalant without a destiny

I refuse to live in the past
worried that every decision will be like the last
I refuse to worry about tomorrow
Let tomorrow worry about tomorrow

I refuse the stereotypical
when being different is much more beautiful

I refuse to build walls, that i cannot scale
I refuse to fall, I refuse to fail
I refuse to be ashamed
it's much more daring to proclaim
I refuse to be cold
how else will I break the norm
I refuse to fold...
under pressure
I refuse to lose
I refuse to refuse

EXHORTATION
Roll Call!

Roll Call!
Attend-Hut!
You Ready!
You Ready!
You Ready!

You see the Time is now, you better get your act together
Storms don't ask permission to disrupt the weather
That's why you got to learn to watch and pray
Speak to that mountain to move outta your way
For God is seeking men of Valour, Soldiers
That will pack in the heart His orders, like manila
folders in file cabinets with faith tendencies and
obedience as their habits

For the General of the Universe is enlisting warriors
Front line workmen who can already see themselves
victorious
Because they anticipate their Commander in Chiefs
Glorious Appearing…
Not fearing death because to be absent from the body is to
be present with the Lord
With confessions of loyalty in one accord with the Will of
the Father and filled with the Light of His double-edged
sword, never to be a victim or the recipient of pain for
these are violent men that take territories by force and of
course Bear His Name
And release the weak from the chains of sin and death, the
chains that are because they haven't accepted the Lord

TALENTS VOLUME I

Yet.

These redeemed which are hard-pressed but not crushed,
perplexed but not in despair, Cast down but not
destroyed, persecuted but not forsaken,
never leaving their appointed stations
because they are a Royal Priesthood and a Holy Nation
and their only Mission is His Great Commission.
Proclaiming the good news causing all to stand at
attention,

Listen,
This is Kingdom Business,
Kingdom vision,
this is for Warriors, Victorious, Kingdom Living
Not for the faint of heart
You better count the Cost
You may suffer loss
Get ready to carry your cross
Are you ready to drink His Cup?
Can you fellowship in His Sufferings
When those who you love turn against you,
Will you never give up?

This is the generation of them that seek Him
A generation of sold out God Pleasers
To Live is Christ, to die is Gain
As Long as I bring Glory to His Name
To Live is Christ, to die is Gain
As Long as His Kingdom is all that Remains
True Christian Soldiers, MAN YOUR BATTLE STATIONS!
THE TIME IS NOW,
ROLL CALL!

INTERLUDES

INTERLUDES

Mercy

A big question mark comes to mind
When You've just rescued me from my latest bind
When I'm deep in my dysfunction, wallowing in my sin
I seem to neglect You
And Your opinion I don't seek to find
Your approval gets overridden by mine
And your Word gets left behind
Even though I say to myself "this time I've really done it,
Committed another unspeakable crime"
I always seem to end up just fine
And If I could get a hold of a tape of my life
Pop it in the VCR and press rewind
I would find evidence so incriminating,
It would make me wanna do time
But the fact of the matter is that such a record does not exist
For Your Blood already took care of this
And even how your Blood came to be shed
So that every fault, every sin could be dismissed
Still perplexes me….insists once again the big question
What Kind of Love is this?
I must have missed, the reason, overlooked the qualities that make me worthy
Then it becomes plain as day,
 It's because of Gods Mercy!

In the Time of Adversity

In the time of adversity
It seems like you're the first
to be targeted with the increased intensity
Of the fire that's supposed to purge the worst in me,
release the unwanted debris, which so easily besets this
journey, Not to mention this enemy tries to steal,
kill and destroy your destiny but even though He can't
win he keeps testing me, to see if I know the Truth has set
me free or if I'm just perpetuating a counterfeit level of
maturity.

But how come the invisible seems more real to me, the
battle in my mind bubbling like wine, this voice tryna
corrupt what I'm inclined to do, to say, to be while the
Spirit is tryna liberate every dream. Manifest Powerful
Rivers outta my tiny streams. Buy the truth and Sell it not,
for Wisdom is the key that determines every continuation
and every stop or in other words whether you move
forward or return to the same spot…..

INTERLUDES

Life

Life is not measured by how many breathes you take
but by how many moments take your breath away
how many things can keep your passions at bay
and leave you blank-eyed, wide-mouthed with nothing to say

Tomorrow's not promised so make the best of today
cuz what's around what you see will pass like hair color turning to gray

That's why you should exercise your knees and pray
and ask God to show you the way

There's a time to work and a time to play
A time to be focused and a time to stray
A time to rebel and a time to obey
Then when time runs out, we return to clay

TALENTS VOLUME I
The Race does not go to the swift

The race does not go to the swift,
But to he that endureth to the end.
Sometimes steel isn't judged by what it can hold,
But by how much it can bend.
There are some doors that open,
That don't care If you walk or crawl,
But just that you make it in,
Because the One who propped it open had,
Already decided you win.
The Journey is not about the outward reward,
But about bringing out the prize within.
The treasure in earthen vessel that's hidden deep within the skin.
You see the Time is now, you better get your act together.
Storms don't ask permission to disrupt the weather.
That's why you gotta learn to watch and pray.
Speak to that mountain to move outta your way.
For God is seeking men of Valour, Soldiers
That will pack in the heart His orders, like manila
Folders in file cabinets with faith tendencies and obedience
As their habits.
For the General of the Universe is enlisting warriors.
Front like workmen who can already see themselves victorious.
Because they anticipate their Commander in Chiefs
Glorious Appearing....

INTERLUDES

Poetically Inclined

If you ask me why I'm a Soldier,
it's because I put my Life on these lines.
When I say I'm a pilot, I allow you to come fly my skies.
The products of my pen create destinations for your
arrival, producing settings and backdrops that rival
natural existence.
That's because you didn't know that my words have
always existed,
Enlisted on a writing slate made for my metaphors and my
"for instances."
For instance this burning desire within my fingers that
produce corresponding sparks.
These words on this page are just my scorch marks.
The conversations in my head that talk.
Personified characters that walk.
Meter and structure go out the window.
Haiku's and convention no longer linger,
because invention makes its own final statement
like Jerry Springer.
Makes mention brings attention and produces intentional
assimilation.
Attend hut!
Now be at ease
but don't stop listening.
A good soldier hangs on every word,
even if I'm whispering.
These lines are in my blood there's no other way to get rid
of them. They echo through the recesses of my conscience
intertwined outside your reaches;
secrets that walk, and impeaches your own words,
leaving you speechless.
Are you sure you ready for Real Talk?

LOVE

Eros
(or ; érōs),

Also called marital love, is passionate love, with sensual desire and longing. The Modern Greek word "erotas" means "(romantic) love"

LOVE
And So The Journey Begins...

As I behold the look in her eyes,
trying to gain access into the window of her soul.
Enchanting yet unpredictable, knowing is my goal.
Discovering a piece of this diamond much more precious than gold,
Like the intricate folds of an Origami Flower
Lovely as a Rose.

Bright as a Sunflower
with a beauty untold,
a radiance and glow
that was made from a different Mold.

She has this power that I'm determined to take hold,
to know,
to show,
that seems to flow to bestow its
essence on its behold-er
as He-Beholds-Her
and knock the chip off of his shoulder...

So He wants to BE the one who HOLDS her
to gain access to the intricates of her folder
such as the brightness of her smile that floods his darkness
and the warmth of her beauty as she leans on his shoulder

The sweet melody of her voice, and confidence in her step
The crystal in her eyes like fine china that's been carefully kept
To Give Praises to the One Above who spent that extra time to mold her
but only if he can gain access to this folder

TALENTS VOLUME I

Only if he has the boldness and perseverance to hold her
the sensitivity and gentleness and strength
to not give up the chase when it looks like he's not reaping
because as the journey begins, know that your role may be principally a sower

But remember that in due time you shall reap if you faint not
because the best apples are always at the top of the tree
but rarely can the giraffe reach them while he's on his knees
So he must climb to his feet and work for that precious prize that's above the leaves...

As he is so pleasantly intrigued
He notices he doesn't really know her
He and her have never met
In fact he hasn't come across her yet

She is the substance of his hope
The recipient of a conversation he never spoke
The prelude to His Dreams
The result of his emptying streams
of desires
the kindling of a burning fire
that drives a quest that's never tiring

Like a twin separated from its other half at birth
He knows she exists
She visits him through the halls of his mind
leaving him clues
one at a time like sips

LOVE

There's a connection
that's partially ripped
that's why he's on this trip
on this journey without a script
to find
a ray that would
lead to the beacon
that shines on him while he's sleeping

and so...

The Journey Begins...

TALENTS VOLUME I
Beauty in View

Whenever I come upon your angelic presence
time just stands still and for a moment
I think that Heaven has just allowed me a taste

When I feel your warmth and radiance
I know it's the rising of the smile on your face
As I behold the timeless glow of your eyes
like the stars in Outer Space

And the gentle breeze made by your wings
as you move with grace
My heart begins to misplace beats
without a trace and run rapidly
as if in a race

An Olympic game, all in reaction to that beautiful name
Sometimes lightning can strike twice
but I think Love has hit me three times

Fried my sense of direction and lighting up every section
of my collection of thoughts, wrought by your reflection
into my eyes
and your brightness into my skies

So I rise, floating on air
because your fragrance has put me there
Your buttermilk baby skin as smooth
as the waters before they get troubled
as subtle as the way your lips affect me double...

LOVE

It's Only Been a Minute

It's only been a minute, but I've had the chance to study you,
To look past your outer appearance, to discern the inner you.

Something inside of you, caused me to take a second look,
My spirit took a hold of it, like a fish on a fishing hook.

Like a sudden flash of light, Am I the only one who saw that?
Whatever it was, so mesmerizing, it caused me to take a step back.

Now it's only been a minute,
but that's all it takes to find that "Good Thing,"

That missing rib from my side,
That helper, help-meet, I've been waiting for my whole life.

So do you meet the criteria, I saw your shine, what's inside,
But we can only burn as one candle, if we agree and walk with one stride.

Are you Saved, are we equally yoked,
are you Spirit-Filled, are you Blood Soaked?

Do you believe in Covenant, Truth and Love?
First and foremost do you cherish your covenant,
with your Bridegroom from above?

TALENTS VOLUME I

Are you into family, and being the Glory at my right hand?
Are you a Prayer warrior? Can I lean on you, when it's hard for me to stand?

What is your purpose, what is your destiny, Is God the Captain of your ship?
Do you honor Him with your actions, the words of your lips?

Do you know you were created to Worship?
Do you value being pure above what this culture presses?

Is your private time with Jesus better than any man's caresses?
Is your intimacy with your Saviour the Love-making you look forward to?

Is being a Proverbs 31 Woman,
and Love and Joy and Peace your primary fruits?

These may seem like alot of questions, but they're the ones which fuel this quest,
There's nothing I will ask of you, that I don't expect of myself.

It may take much more than a minute for me to know the real you,
but in this span of one minute, this is what my mind is considering asking you.

It only takes a minute to see your light,
and decide if I want to get to know you.

LOVE
If Only One Moment with You Baby

Moments come once in time
Lasting for an instance but can never rewind
And no other chance you can find
To repeat a moment lost in time

Every Waking Moment
Even when I'm asleep I'm thinking of ways to make you smile
Every Precious Moment
Thinking of you
Always seem to last a while

So Heavenly cuz I know Heaven has taken time out of the equation
Lent me a Gift
Such a Beautiful Lady
When I start to think of you baby

I ……………………………………….
For a sec there I lost words to say
Tryna catch my breath before you retake my breath away

Where was I, Moments,
Moments that you want to stay
Moments that you pray for
You wait for
You create space for
And plan your day for

That's the kind of moments I experience when I'm with you
Surreal moments that create lasting memories

That's why I wanna spend my precious moments with you

If ONLY ONE MOMENT WITH YOU BABY......

Moments come once in time
Lasting for an instance but can never rewind
And no other chance you can find
To repeat a moment lost in time......

LOVE
Just thinking about you again

It's become a habit of mine
Thinking about you time after time
Whispers of you filling up my mind with lovely thoughts
Erasing the empty areas and the lonely spots
Listening to your messages left on my phone, just to hear your voice
More priceless to me than a Bentley and two Rolls Royce
Looking at your smile in a picture
Reminds me of how the way you make me feel has become a fixture
Of joy and happiness so infectious
And the look in your eyes so precious
I say to myself what did I do to deserve such a blessing
That God has afforded me his princess
To become my queen
It seems like he reached into my sub-conscious and took her from my dreams

Wondering what you're doing at this present moment has become my song
Feeling like every moment away from you is way too long
Sometimes your presence becomes so very strong
That I can't tell which way is right or which way is wrong
Other times reality behaves so cruel reminding me you're gone

But not too far away
Just absent from my present space
But present in the secret place
You've taken in my heart
Illuminating my skies brighter than any star

TALENTS VOLUME I

In outer space
Leaving just a trace
Of your Beautiful face….
So that I can start thinking about you ….again

LOVE
"MASTERPIECE"

She had the canvas, I Just Painted on it.
A work of Art so masterfully created that nothing in this world could replicate. That's why I knew she was one of a kind the very first time my brush spoke to me.

1st Stroke, A preparation called the color introduction. This line of color blended so well, but I still could not tell or make out any saturation…and so I set another "appointment" where I could better work in my element to see if this material could ever produce a specific pictorial known as the Color Of Love.

2nd Stroke, I painted Conversation to lay the foundation, revealing her Intellectual side, before I got more personal to try out the Yellows and Grays…the shady parts of her life, to find out what produced her Blues and dismays.

3rd Stroke, Intent to erase these Blues, I indulged her with Reds; Like roses, breakfast in bed and beauty treatments for her Pretty Head.

4th Stroke, this seems like a stroke of luck, cuz as I continued to scratch the surface, she responded to every touch of my brush in every way blending smoothly, allowing me to "paint" deeper.

5th Stroke, if only you could see Her,
Her mesmerizing Black outline expressing her figure And that Ivory smile, ooh that Silver style keeps her glowing and that Purple won't keep those hips from showing, Or that bold Black hair from flowing,
And even those Hazel eyes….so adoring

TALENTS VOLUME I

6th Stroke, a sight to be seen,
The chemistry between the two of us and no gaps in between. By now a lot of Green, but I do not mind. What's mines is hers, nevertheless Nothing is more priceless, no amount of money measures up to what I feel inside

7th Stroke, I left no area untouched; the number of completion...perfection, That's because I got to search every inch of her soul. My racing heart would not slow down until a final stroke of Gold took her Ring-finger in a choke-hold

Framed: A Masterpiece made complete because you and me were destined to be. Art unrivaled by the likes of Picasso, Davince, and Van Gogh, For our Love is a Work too valuable to put in an art show. That's why this picture remains a fixture on the Wall of my Heart where it will never get sold.

LOVE
On My Mind

On my mind like the refreshing dew of the morning
Elevating my mood like the Gentle Wind that keeps me soaring

Illuminating my countenance like the distant shine of the stars on a clear evening
Gracing my presence, so real, but I think I'm dreaming
Invisible, but I know it's more than just a feeling
cuz nothing else but this feeling can get me reeling
can get my heartbeat to hit the ceiling
speeding faster than a formula 1 race
every time your face appears in my mind
like a pop-up ad that I don't mind

When the thoughts and reminders of you take center stage
I feel like I'm reading the end of a book that I never wanna turn the last page
Freeze every moment like Peter Pan never wanting to age
Causing reactions not normal but okay
Like talking before I even know what to say
Or fiending even though I've never been drugged
But this reverb leaves a trace like a shooting star forced to remain in place
An echo so special its borderline incredible
Not even legible
Worthy of a pedestal

Your voice that is
Makes me realize
Like the bubbles in soda, the fizz
I need you like the answers to a quiz
Like a burger without fries, I don't feel complete

TALENTS VOLUME I

Like a car without the seats
Or a song with no beat
Like a vehicle with an oil leak
I feel a draining in my heart
Like the beats have left
Or the feeling after realizing the alarm that you forgot to set..........

Girl you're doing something to me......I like it

LOVE

Sitting Here

Sitting here trying to find the words to say
Trying to turn the language of the heart
Into something recognizable on a page
Putting together feelings that you cannot name
But only seem to manifest when you think about her name
And so you know the source of what's driving you crazy
It's a certain beautiful lady
Her eyes, her lips, her skin, her hips
Her curves, her smile, her nose, her dips
Her voice, her soul, her mind, her grip
Here dance, her grace, her study face
Here arguments, her tendencies, her intuition
Her smile, her gaze, the way she listens
The way her eyes seem to glisten
Creating a star worthy of wishing

And so I'll try, baby just listen:

You see when I say you're beautiful
Something powerful flows outta my heart
A breathtaking phenomenon that ranks way off the charts
If you knew the adoration in my being
Every time I look at you
The many dreams I keep seeing
Because they are all of you
The recollection of feelings so deep and true,
The stars in the sky can't compare to you
If you could see my point of view
How you got me going crazy
Because you call me baby
Then maybe, pretty lady
Full of Beauty so Beautiful

Beauty Composition 1

Your Beautiful

Much more than my words could ever show
How can I portray this vision that I see
How does one express the effect of the rays of sun
How can one describe the fabrics of each sunrise
to someone who has no eyes

Well you know what I can....Number one: Your Smile

Way more than eyes can see
it produces a perception that even the blind can see
A warmth that can be felt so pleasantly
like the gentle kiss of the wind on summer leaves
Radiating such energy better described as eye candy
More beautiful than the black and gold sands of Hawaii
like kryptonite causing weak knees and elevated heart beats
like diamonds and pearls
like being elevated from the nosebleed to the best seats

Your Smile.

Beauty Composition 2

Your eyes

More breathtaking than any sunrise
Your eyes
as Captivating as the Eagle as it takes off to fly
Your eyes
they glisten like the brightest star in the sky
Mesmerizing
Hypnotizing
Specializing in Beauty
Piercing through
demanding attention, bringing all eyes on you
You see your eyes encompass the very glow
of your essence
and Light up my world more than birthday and Christmas
presents
combined,

Your eyes.

Beauty Composition 3

Your Spirit

The Real You
The Cream Feeling
The Crème de la Crème
Where your true beauty resides

Your Spirit

The inner dwelling place
of the treasure known as you
What makes up the essence of
your presence
and Blesses me
Like a banging meal,
Can I have Seconds?

Your Spirit

Where you Worship God
and are alive to your Creator
The most important part of you
What makes you so Beautiful
Immune to age
Filled with Praise
because a Virtuous Woman Loves the Lord
Just like,

Your Spirit

LOVE

Loving Eyes

So much has changed and I don't know when it happened
but the way I look at you is different
because I'm looking at you through Loving eyes

What I see has changed from what I saw
What i see is me and you and you and I
and me has become we and just I has become us
Two as One
together
Intertwined as the strands of a leather
belt...I
I can't explain why looking at you
causes my insides to melt
like butter...yes
Butter cream is how sweet your presence is to me.
This is what I see
Because I'm looking at you through Loving eyes

Man how do i describe this airy feeling
of floating on clouds and this uneasiness
that i can't explain out loud
This is so new, yet a little deja vu
my heart has always known, but my mind is just getting
introduced to you...

TALENTS VOLUME I

Agape
(or, agápē),

The Pure and Holy Love of God.
Unconditional,
Self-less Love,
The Love of Christ.

TALENTS VOLUME I

Love

A Love that knows no bounds
A Love that existed before time
Love that brought into existence
A Love that has no Limits

Love that hand-knit the heart
Piece by piece with a little bit of Heaven in part
The Love that fuels the stars
And keeps the notes hanging on the bars
of a sweet melody and gives the harmony its Liberty
Love that hung the Moon in the heavenlies
that creates inseparable friends from Enemies

Love that unlocks the Mystery of His Will
and causes the Lions mouth to be still
Love that erases the frozen tundra's chills
and causes the addict to drop those pills
causes the tears to spill from their eyes
cuz this feeling that arrests them is
Greater than any High

Love that is His very Nature
That can't be bought by any wager
Love that permeates through this paper
Love so Powerful in can Never waver

Love that turns Master into Servant
Love that endured Calvary with no deterrent
Love that sacrificed a Son
And Conformed two wills into One
(not my will, but they Will be done)

TALENTS VOLUME I

Love with the power to resurrect
And bring eternity into retrospect
Love that is the same today, yesterday, and tomorrow

Agape

LOVE
Unconditional

How deeply do you Love Me?
I asked my Heavenly Father.

He replied, "More than you'll ever know my child."
Well what if I tell a lie? Will you stop Loving Me?
What if you enquire of me and I give no Reply?
What if you say Go and I don't even try?
What if I smoke or use Drugs to get High?
What if I sell my Body just to get By?
What if before marriage I sleep with that Guy?
What if I'm not patient?
What if when I raise my hands I'm faking?
What if I don't give but keep taking?
What if I get mad at you?
What if after continuous instruction, I still don't know what to do?
What if I refuse to turn the other cheek?
What if I'm weak?
What if your Kingdom is not the first thing I seek?
What if I ignore you when you speak?
What if I cheat?
What if I get cold feet?
What if I lived the life of a gang-banger on the streets?
Or keep the sin in my life on repeat?
Will you still Love Me the same?

He replied "Yes." That's why I sent my Son,
For your weaknesses, your sins, past, present and future.
For you He came
He did not come to blame or bring you shame,
But he came to reinstate you with the Fathers Last Name
He came so that you could once and for all claim eternal life.

TALENTS VOLUME I

Break the chains and end all strife.
Fix you, make you whole, from the physical to the Spiritual

Yes my Child my Love for you is Unconditional!!

LOVE
The Mystery Called Love

What is Man that you were mindful of him,
Before He was corrupted by this World of Sin?
What is this substance wrought from the depths of the Earth,
That houses this spirit of yours from the day of Birth?
How can clay with the characteristic of dirt,
Possess a treasure way surpassing its worth?
What is this mystery that you knew of first?
That man could receive water and never thirst,
That flesh could be Filled, but never burst,
That the Spirit of God could dwell with the worst,
And the Love of God could remove this Curse….
The Mystery Called Love…

What is Man that thou visiteth,
Of whom, before he existed, you thought
Before the worlds were framed?
You called Him by name, whom in the Garden you sought,
And whom through Calvary you bought,
With the life of the One who came
To endure pain and shame, heal and serve the lame,
All without any claim to fame?
Through whom sin, the flesh, death, Hell and the Grave were tamed.
Even though demons shuddered and rocks quaked
At the mention of His name,
He chose to Humble Himself in obedience,
Even unto the Cross…
How Awesome Is this Mystery Called Love

TALENTS VOLUME I

Man was made a little lower than the Angels,
Yet You bypassed them and crowned him with Glory?
But that's not the end of the story,
You see these earthen vessels,
You entrusted with spreading your message
The Great Commission
No tools, no gimmicks all they had was Your
Words to get man to listen…
"Repent For the Kingdom of Heaven is at Hand"
Jesus Christ of Nazareth has Risen
Believe in your Heart, and Confess with your mouth that
He is Lord
You will receive eternal Life, go from death to Living
And restore that part of you that is Missing

And So the Glory of God is seen among men
His ultimate plan since way before when
God created beings for His own pleasure
But Human Beings he created to share,
In His pleasure,
His presence, and to dwell with Him forever

The Mystery called Love,
That is revealed to those whom He Loves

LOVE
Love...or Like...Love or like love...or just Like?

There's a thin line between love and like

Not really

More like the space between this page and your eyes
You see to most people love is loose terminology
knowing full well that it's just a result of
like imposing in unfamiliar territory
better yet
like
posing
as love
An imitation of a standard way above
its
characteristics
That's why it ends up being said so many times as if
convincing
yourself that it's true
But the reality is that you're not being realistic
Because if it was love you'd know the difference

There's a thin line between love and like

Meaning
Like, crosses a boundary line that inevitably leads to that
pain called heartache
It doesn't hurt to wait, to use this four letter word
Hey if it ain't the real thing
it's better that you let that one get away

There's a thin line between love and like
More like the distance between

TALENTS VOLUME I

the truth and a lie
Although like can become love
it takes way more than
I'm really digging you
way more than a tingling feeling
way more than physical attraction
or silly flirtation
It takes a realization
that if this addition becomes subtraction
it would induce a pain
worse than labor contractions

There's a thin line between love and like

for those who wear their heart on their sleeves
because they've never comprehended
that there's a distinction between the two
or experienced
true
L
O
V
E
Agape
unconditional
You see I found that on my knees
When nothing in existence could fulfill my needs
or fill the emptiness
That I constantly tried to feed
with
counterfeits
But instead they created fits of rejection
infusions of transfusions of the

LOVE

the wrong blood type
Because the type i needed was
the Blood of Christ
and the healing I needed
of these heart pains
was by His Stripes
and even the new Breath I've Needed
was His Spirit
I'm on cloud nine not because of
an infatuation
but a graduation from
superficial
to Love
from just foolish attraction to satisfaction

Godly Love
The real thing
no imitation
It does not exist on a thin line
because it's so much greater
it erases all limitations.

TALENTS VOLUME I
How You Gonna Sing About Love

How You Gonna Sing about Love and not Sing about Me
Don't you know that its genesis came from Above?
How You Gonna Talk about Love and not Talk about Me
Is it possible to repeat something you've never heard speak?
How You Gonna Say You Love, and yet you don't know Me
That's like writing an in-depth biography of someone you've never met
That's like saying the water's cold but you've never got your feet wet
How you expect to find Love, when you haven't found Me
Because I am Love, the source of Love, True Love is in Me
How you say you Love, but everyone is your enemy,
How dare you when I gave my Life for all with no partiality
How you gonna hear my Gospel of Love and not feed the hungry, care for the sick or give to the poor?
Then have the audacity to pray to me asking for more....
Money, more blessings, and not for the ones you ignore?
Do you really think that having My mind, means keeping your own?
God is not mocked do you think I am lying when I say you reap what you sow?
Money, Cars, Houses, and Popularity are all your after
But what good is all of these vanities without the Love of the Master

LOVE

A generation stuck on materialism and never content; always wanting more
When living, walking, talking, like me is what you should be living for

So let me draw you an illustration, and maybe you'll see the demarcation
When you don't know how to use something, you read the instruction manual
So how can you throw around the word Love when you haven't consulted the manual?
Do you not think the manufacturer knows how it works?
It's so much harder to eat soup when instead of a spoon you're using a fork

You see your conversation is Love's imitation
Your three words, an impersonation of Heavens indoctrination
A corruption of Heavens instruction
A reproductive malfunction of its function
An irritation of His intention
A Mockery of a perfect original
And a presumption compared to Gods initial

Don't you know that Love is not just a word, it's spiritual?
Not to be taken literal or used as experimental
A song with no need for words, It's like an instrumental
It's supplied by a God who named it unconditional
And gave it the power to touch every individual

So when you sing about Love, Be careful to mention The Source because the rocks have no problem taking your place

The Search is Over

To need someone more than you need air
To need someone like a 2nd floor needs stairs
That can take that heart that you thought was broke beyond repair
And turn it into a heart that still cares
You never thought you could Love again
Or let someone get closer than a friend

You never thought, your most intimate feelings you could share
Partly because you thought no one else
Could understand or bear

You've come to the conclusion that Life isn't fair
And you had all but given up on prayer
Because you never expected anyone to be there
Let alone someone to number you hairs
Or further more bottle those tears
So much pain, it hurts so much
Like driving automatic when the car uses a clutch
You never thought an invisible touch could feel so safe
Or that anyone could relate

But you find out that He is not just anyone
For He is Gods Son
And that all this time you've been searching for the wrong "one"
For His words only bring joy
Like when a baby gets its first toy

LOVE

His presence revives your laughter
And His voice causes your heart to beat faster
Thinking of Him Gives you perfect peace
And His Love knocks you off your feet

This new passion burning within you
Refines you and makes you feel brand new
You can always depend on Him, He's faithful and true
Trustworthy, and caring, and guess what, He's totally into you

He gives you back your self-worth
Cuz he's was the one who said you were beautiful….first

TALENTS VOLUME I

SALVATION

SALVATION

The Battlefield

This thing is real.

An organized front and campaign from High Places.
An all out assault from invisible spaces. Taking out your weapons capabilities from inside your fort, with an enemy not using or deterred by conventional weapons. An enemy so relentless that it could lose its legs and keep on stepping on your mission objectives coupled with its allied force of life lessons and camouflaged deception. An enemy with the audacity to cause insurrection in the face of authority that he PALES in comparison.

This thing is real.

An adversary with over 3,000 years of practice and counting that uses spies in every corner to do his scouting. Prefers confrontation using Goliaths and Mountains.

You see this thing is real...

Dwelling on the iniquities of the Fathers to bypass his armor and to get to his sons. The biggest danger to a soldier is not the enemy fire, it's fighting in a war that's already been won; and having no knowledge that it's over. A non-conventional battlefield front because fighting an enemy you can't see, makes you the object of the hunt.

This thing is real...

We wrestle not against flesh and blood, but world systems and patterns, influences, invisible spirits and mindsets. Advanced by radio, movies, internet, and television sets.

TALENTS VOLUME I

Thoughts that originate as fiery darts.
But we have weapons that were Mighty from the start
that annihilate strongholds and pierce through the heart.
Causing devastation to the Kingdom of Darkness that
ranks way off the charts.

Though we suffer violence we take it by Force;
Casting down high things and doctrines that steer men off course,
of the knowledge of God.
Bringing into subjection disobedient thoughts,
Conquering conquerors by the Word Jesus taught,

Because we know this thing is real...

Not based on what you feel but a reality way past feelings,
past your day to day dealings that requires a man of
Warfare. A man of Prayer. Who refuses to entangle himself
with the affairs of this life. The he may please him who
enlisted him, the one with snowy white hair.
This battlefield of the mind, The Battle in the Spirit,
that is not just a momentary conflict, we constantly live it.
Requires Men of Surrendered wills and Faith without
limits. Rich in resolve but poor in spirit. We know this
battle does not go to the swift, nor to the strong,
but to He that endureth and end with a Song
of victory, knowing that He was not on the wrong side
because his Commander in Chief contrary to popular
belief is still Alive. Though he does not see it, the battle
rages on, His God has already revealed that

This Thing Is Real....

SALVATION
Prisoner To Me............No Longer

Going through life, going through the motions
Little dedication, minor devotion
to anything that was close to discretion
flocking to anything that would excite my emotions

Going with the flow is a law unspoken
A roller coaster ride where the brakes are broken
Living for the moment, migrating to the next High
Pummeling to the depths, but still thinking I can fly

Lying, cheating, stealing, deceiving,
pride, jealousy, and blatant disobedience
Alcohol, drugs, sex, money,
the lusts of this Life
The chains that bind me in their endless enterprise
Multiple bars and clubs where I frequent each night
Waking up next to strangers still feeling empty inside

Wreck less abandonment
To me what was wrong was more right
As long as I fed this addiction
Trying everything to numb the effect, make things easier
My own concoctions of homemade Anesthesia
but I could never seem to go under like lying on an operating table
still conscious but not being able to move
feeling every surgical incision but not being able to even send a clue
that I'm trapped inside myself...
I'm not supposed to feel the knife?

Yet I still don't give a....Fight

cuz I'm used to this feeling
There's nothing better is what I'm used to believing

The World said, "Welcome to the Good Life"
A truth distorted
Maybe a couple of Mornings
Then it soon becomes boring
or maybe that's too soft of a description because on the outside
this life looks appealing
but inside I was reeling, chronically bleeding

I was....

A prisoner to me
Bound to satisfying every whim

But no longer
obligated to react to every craving
But no longer
are my eyes dim
But no longer
am I bound to Sin
But no longer
am I trapped in my own skin
Because I gave up that lifestyle
with its momentary pleasures
for eternal incorruptible treasures
I gave up pain and emptiness
for peace in stormy weather

SALVATION

Now I can't say that I have the good life,
but my Soul Is much better
Since I gave my life to Christ
He broke me outta that prison
I'm a living Witness
The Phoenix has risen
No more chains or defeated living
No more fetters
I'm stronger
You see, Now that I'm Free
I'm a Prisoner to Me...No longer

They Encounter

They weep. They Cry. His Blood was spilled.
They hunger. They Thirst. They Shall Be Filled.
He was wounded. He was Bruised.
By His Stripes they are Healed.

They Drank.
They Smoked.

They threw away Those Pills.

He died. He Raised. With His Spirit they are Sealed.
Every sin. Every slip. With His Life He foot the Bill.
Every Fear. Every Worry. With His Voice He Stilled.
The Verdict.
The Penalty.
He Alone Repealed.

Love. Joy. Peace. To those who Yield.
Purpose. Identity. He Alone Instills.
Good. Acceptable. Perfect Will.
He Tore.
The Veil.
The Father Revealed.

The Word. Made Flesh. Glory Concealed.
They Bow. They Confess. They Kneel.
They've tasted. They've seen. God is Real.
Sir.
We would.
See Jesus!

SALVATION

Armageddon

As both sides emerge over the hill side
an empty expanse of grass separates the two
An eerie calm ensues as in enters proof of what the battle
is for

Each sizes up the opposition as each banner is raised
One side fully confident, the other is Afraid
One side full of hope, the other full of rage

The enemies of the Cross, the adversary ready to engage
but not realizing that One had already set the stage
Thinking that this war he would wage
would give him final victory
That the ruler of this Age would take what rightfully
belongs to me

Not realizing that the battle hinges more on what he
cannot see
Because if he really considered the cost
of what would be lost
He would not have rebelled and
left his first estate
thinking he himself could become Supreme Potentate

The Deceiver, the one ultimately deceived
A vendetta against the inheritance Man received
A tragedy of eternal proportions because
he truly believed he won
when violence had its way and Nailed the
Prince of Peace to a Tree
Bloodied for all to see

TALENTS VOLUME I

He really believed in his own arrival
as the new king of kings
Until he watched the resurrected Lord
leaving with Death and Hells Keys
and all things being placed under his feet

Even though he had read it Centuries upon centuries before
Of his eventual defeat
in prophecy after prophecy
he still refused to believe to concede

That the seed of a woman would bruise his head
The Son of David, Jesus Christ

And so brings us to his last attempt
to interfere with the Lambs Wedding
A battle for the existence of the Saints
A Groom returns for His Bride
at this place, this valley called Armageddon

The accuser of the brethren failed to foresee
that on the side of humanity is Jehovah Nissi
Glorious riding on a White Horse
descending from the Sky
Inscribed on His Thigh
Lord of Lords and King of Kings
in all Splendor and Might

That Serpent of old
that was bold enough to take on Heaven from Earth
to ascend higher

SALVATION

Finally realizes that he is destined for the Lake of Fire
His blatant ignorance of God's Word
he could not afford
to play with a double-edged sword
Because he would have known that
the battle was over when God declared
to His people,
the Battle is Not Yours, It is the Lords!

TALENTS VOLUME I
Valley of Decision

Standing in the moment, moment, moment
of truth, as the inhibitions that bind you slowly release,
release, release
and the reverberation that you hear
of chains falling at your feet are drowned out by a thump,
thump, thump,
drumbeat of your heart, as if the finish-line has now
turned into the start.

Go, go, go,
is the response after the gun
before the final whistle, is when this game must
be won except this race against time is all in my mind,
mind...mind?
I think that was all in my head,
because still what was before me is still ahead.

What is this drawing? What is this decision?
What is this calling? Why must I listen?
What is this vision that I keep seeing, of me walking?...But
I'm sitting?
And I'm glad that echo stopped or did it?

It seems like whatever's said is twice and three times read
and
replayed over and over again especially for my ears and
what is up
with this valley that just appeared with signs that point to
decisions,
there's so many people here.

SALVATION

Signs that say no more fear, no more tears
He'll never put more on you than you can bear,
Draw near, draw near, He cares, He cares, He cares,
He cares for you, and you shall know the Truth,
because He has walked in more than a mile of your shoes.
He shed, He shed, He shed His blood for you.
Then it all becomes so clear, I've been chosen,
I'm no longer frozen in this valley because I've
just been shared the Good News.
I accept this transfer from death to Living,
and the gift that God the Father has given.
Eternal Life because Jesus Christ has risen,
broken chains and release from life's prison.
I've finally made my decision.

I Believe!

Lamb of God

He was led
Robe ripped to shreds
He was led
Wounded
He was led
Bruised
Amidst stripes for healing,
Still He was led

Crown of thorns jammed into his head
He was led
Not a word he said
As He was led
His back so red
From scars that formed pits
And reservoirs of the Blood He shed

He was led
Through the Via De La Rosa
Carrying that old rugged cross
Knowing that He was carrying this burden in our stead
Still He was led

Never taking His eyes off the stony road ahead
Even when His knees buckled from the load He bared
As His sweat seemed to turn to blood
He was led

He was led through the crowds of people
Who still demanded He be crucified…
Even though He was innocent, still no one cared

SALVATION

Give us the murderer Barnabas Instead
Still ringing, ringing, ringing in His head

Still as by beacon he was led
Up that road of Calvary
With the resolve of a Lion
Of Judah that is with no dread
Onto that Hill He was led

The Lamb led to the slaughter
Slain before the Foundations of the World
The Lamb of God the full embodiment
Of the Fathers Love unfurled
Nailed to the Cross He Carried
So that you and I wouldn't be eternally buried
Nails in His arms stretched out wide
Nails in His feet, Pierced on His Side
As the enemy thought defeat
"Father forgive them for they know not
What they're doing", He Speaks

As the Blood and water kept flowing
10,000 legions of Angels He could Have Called
But still He stayed on that Cross
Eli, Eli, My God, My God He Cried,
It is finished He hung His Head
And for a moment the World thought all was lost.......
….He Died……………….
But that's not the end of the story
But what they had not foreseen
That at a time of three,
Perfection
The number of the trinity

What all of history had been waiting for
And had not ever been done before
No grave could keep, yet alone a tomb
The Son of God, from Living.
For on the Third Day He had risen
The King of Glory
Is Living
All Dominion
All Authority
To Him is Given
As He Ascended
For all to see
The Hour Has Come
For all to believe
To receive
The Hope of this World
Will return
With all Power in his hands

….AND NOW BEHOLD THE LAMB.

SALVATION

Altar Call

So excited yet so unsure
Like being at a party but not ready to get on the dance floor
Going through the motions in your head
Fueled by the words that were said
And the emotions that were read
But instead
Surrendering your desire, so that you can be led
Making room, so that you can be fed
That's what the preacher said

I heard.
I know that Jesus paid a price
What does it mean to give Him your Life?
How do you surrender all and not think twice

You're asking me to walk down that aisle
For me, that's just as easy as treading on ice
My feet seem to agree and hold together as in a vice

There goes the preacher again
Why won't he keep quiet?
"But if you don't it's like trusting your future to a roll of the dice
Secure your eternity, a no won't suffice"
All these eyes, the people like nice…
But how do I know that when I walk they won't judge me
Are they truly genuine do they really want to get to know me?
They say come join the family
But I'm a little skeptical

TALENTS VOLUME I

Something is telling me to step out and see
Come try Me and see if I'm not all that you need
Could it be Him....He's speaking to me?
Naw I must be hearing things
Why won't this service end it seems like they waiting on me
Well I wanna believe, but...there it goes again, I hear His voice ring

Come unto me, give me your hand
I promise I'll never Leave
I'll walk with you and make you free
I'll brighten your eyes so that you can see
Come my child and receive my peace

That does it, how can I resist
This Jesus they talk about …
when He promises all this…

Okay here goes; I'll go to that altar
Because I'm a child in desperate need of a Father

And it's not because of what the preacher said
But it's because of Jesus, I'm no longer afraid

SALVATION
What does it really mean to be a Christian?

I thought it meant to be a witness.
Not just calling oneself one,
but corresponding actions supporting that confession.
I shouldn't have to tell you but you should deduce it
just from your first impression....of me,
I mean Acts chapter 1:8 seems to back up this statement
but lately as i look at the condition of the Church today,
The called out company of believers formerly known as "the Way,"
it looks like the majority are just in the way
instead of pointing to the Way,
don't forget the Truth and the Life.

What happened to the "for me to live is Christ, to die is gain"?
What happened to the rejoicing when you go through pain,
just because you've been privileged to fellowship in His Suffering?
What happened to I've not already attained?
Counting all things loss and but dung to win Christ?
I mean didn't He say foxes have holes and birds have nest
but the Son of Man has no where to lay
His Head, so why does his followers today
have the audacity to speak "if they don't put me in a hotel with grapes I won't come preach?"
What happened to fire shut up in my bones?
What happened to total surrender, my body is not my own?
What happened to not my own will, but Your Will be done?

Or did we forget the most important Audience of ONE?
How did the Gospel get so watered down and distilled with all this selfish gain?
I thought we're not supposed to love the things of this world, So why does your dedication to the Lord hinge on whether your rich or poor?
Whether you get that raise, that car, that house with the hardwood floors?
What ever happened to endure hardship as a good soldier in Christ,
A soldier that doesn't entangle himself with the affairs of this life?
Focusing on souls because the Harvest is plentiful, the Harvest is Ripe?
If you were thrown in the Lions den or the Furnace's fire, would you.......

SALVATION
Call to Salvation

Are you ready to Believe?
Are you sure that If you died tonight you would spend eternity in Heaven with the Lord?

"For all have sinned, and come short of the Glory of God" (Romans 3:23)

"For the wages of sin is death… (Romans 6:23)

…**But**…

"The Gift of God is Eternal Life through Jesus Christ our Lord!" (Romans 6:23)

Why?

"For God So Loved the world that He gave His only Begotten Son, so that whosoever believeth in Him should not perish but have everlasting life" (John 3:16)

How?

"That if thou shalt confess with thy mouth the Lord Jesus, and shalt believe in thine heart that God hath raised him from the dead, thou shalt be saved" (Romans 10: 9-10)

"For whosoever shall call upon the name of the Lord shall be saved" (Romans 10:13).

If you have never accepted Jesus Christ as your Lord and Saviour, today is the day that you can receive eternal life and get your eternity set and secure. He shed His Blood to wash away ALL of your sins. For under Gods Law, the penalty for sin is death but because of His amazing Love for you and I, God the Father sent His only Son to take our place on that cross. For the Bible says "Greater love hath no man than this, that a man lay down his life for his friends" (John 15:13). Jesus took the death sentence for you and I and died on the cross; however on the third day the Spirit of God raised Him from the Dead! He defeated death, hell, and the grave and went to prepare a place for you and I to spend eternity with him forever! All you have to do is Believe that Jesus Christ is the Son of God and confess it with your mouth, and you are Saved! Invite Him to come into your life right now, to be Lord over your life so that you can truly start living the wonderful life that God has intended for you to live.

Pray this prayer out loud:

Lord Jesus, I thank you for your Love. I thank you for coming into this world and dieing for me, but not only dieing, but raising for me. I truly believe with all my heart that you are the Son of God and so I ask that you would come into my life right now. I know that I am a sinner and so I ask that you would wash me with your

SALVATION

blood so that I may become a new creation. Fill me with your Holy Spirit, give me a hunger for your word, give me a passion for the lost. I accept you as my Lord and Savior and I declare without a shadow of a doubt that right now I AM SAVED!!

Congratulations you are now a Child of God, welcome to the Family!!!

If you prayed this prayer, send me a message at

TalentsVol1@gmail.com

TALENTS VOLUME I

Acknowledgements

To my Heavenly Father, the Talent Giver, all the Glory, Honor and Credit belongs to You, Thank You! To My Lord and Savior Jesus Christ, Thank You, for I know with all of my Heart that You supernaturally activated this gifting in my life. To the Holy Spirit, words cannot express what you mean to me and what happened when you came into my life in 2003, Thank You!

I want to thank my sister Yewande Adeyemi for pushing me to get this project started, that initial push was the catalyst to get this train rolling, Love You; and my brother in Christ Jayson S. Williams for catching a hold of my vision and motivating me to "step my game up." There are divine connections that occur to push you towards your destiny. I truly believe God has joined us together with similar spirits.

To all those who supported me with kind words and listened to my spoken word over the years,

Thank You!

For Speaking Engagements, Performance Requests, or all other correspondence please write to:

TalentsVol1@gmail.com

http://talents.ws

www.ingramcontent.com/pod-product-compliance
Lightning Source LLC
Chambersburg PA
CBHW070501100426
42743CB00010B/1710